Your Book of Paper Folding

The YOUR BOOKS Series

Your Book of
PAPER FOLDING

Vanessa and Eric de Maré

With diagrams by Vanessa de Maré

FABER AND FABER
London

First published in 1968
by Faber and Faber Limited
3 Queen Square London WC1
Reprinted 1971
Printed in Great Britain by
Latimer Trend & Co Ltd Plymouth

ISBN 0 571 08446 x

745.54

Contents

Introduction

Paper was invented in China about 1,800 years ago. The Arabs learned how to make it from Chinese prisoners of war, and it was introduced to Europe by the Moors after they had invaded Spain. It seems to have reached England in the fourteenth century, but it was not made here until Tudor times, when it began to replace parchment and vellum for books and documents.

The making of objects by folding paper is as old as paper itself. Such objects were first used in the East for magical and religious ceremonies. The Chinese made paper models of houses, furniture and other things to be burned during funeral rites so that the spirits of the dead might have all they needed in their after-lives. Mock paper money tucked into red envelopes was sometimes burned at weddings to bring prosperity to the married couple. For centuries past in Japan people have attached paper ornaments to the gifts they present at ceremonies like weddings and birthdays, and the different ways in which the folds go have different meanings. Many creatures and flowers have symbolic meanings in the East. In Japan the Crane means Good Luck and the Frog stands for Love and Fertility.

In Japan paper folding is called Origami and there it is regarded as an art. The simple folded object is considered to be superior to that which is cut or glued. The more simple the method the more perfect the design is thought to be. In the West paper folding is not regarded as an art but only as a minor craft and a hobby. However it may be regarded, it certainly gives pleasure to many people.

Most of the models in this book are traditional designs from China and Japan. They have been folded by both children and adults for hundreds of years, being taught by one generation to the next. Among the few models here which are not oriental in origin are Mr. Randlett's delightful Mouse and Angel Fish, and also the Gift Box, which we learned from a friend.

Section I explains how to use paper and tools, and it gives the meanings of the symbols on the diagrams. Most of these symbols were designed by Akira Yoshizawa, an Origami expert of Tokio, and they are now in general use all over the world. Section I also explains simple folds and then the more complicated Bases from which many models are begun. Sections 2 to 7 show how to make the models themselves. They are arranged in order from the easy to the more difficult ones. The models can be made twice the size shown in the drawings, or larger still, although the smaller their size the more charming they often look.

You may be able to think of different ways of displaying the models. For example, you could make a flight of birds and hang them with thread from a system of thin rods of wood of varying lengths so that they swing and move in a draught of air. Such a system is called a Mobile. Or you may try to invent new models of your own. That is not easy but it is fun to try.

1

Materials and Methods

Papers and Tools

Thin crisp paper is best. Sheets from a pad of writing paper can be used to learn all the folds and will make most of the models. Special Origami paper from Japan can be bought at many stationers and book-shops in packets of fifty ready-cut squares coloured on one side and in six different colours. You can also cut your own squares from all kinds of paper, suiting the paper to the object you are making. Coloured wrapping paper, typing paper, some wallpapers, strong brown paper, coloured poster paper and the end-papers used in book-binding can all be used. Waxed paper is ideal for models to float or to fill with water.

Work on a flat, hard surface such as a table top. Because paper tends to stretch, do not fold it in the air. Fold with the paper flat on the table and sharpen the creases with the thumb or a finger-nail. Match all the points neatly. Sharp points are needed to make beaks, tails and legs. The beauty of the finished model depends on the accuracy of the first few folds. If you have made mistakes and want to start a model from the beginning again, take a fresh piece of paper rather than using the old, tired piece with all its creases.

A ruler, a pencil and a pair of scissors with sharp points will be needed. A set-square with forty-five degree angles is not essential but it is useful for marking out your own squares.

A square with sides of five to seven inches is the usual Origami size, but you may find larger squares easier when you start—perhaps with

11

sides of eight, or even ten, inches. Then try to make smaller models.

Marking in with pencil some of the lines and writing letters, A, B, C and so on at the different points may be a help when you start.

Eyes can be marked on the finished model with a pen or pencil, black or coloured. A paper punch can also be used.

A paper guillotine makes the cutting of squares very easy, but you can also make your own squares with pencil and scissors like this:

1. Fold point A on to point B and make a crease along the line CD.

2. Cut away the bottom part of the paper along line C to AB with scissors. Make sure you are left with a perfectly straight line at the bottom of the triangle.

3. Open out the square of paper.

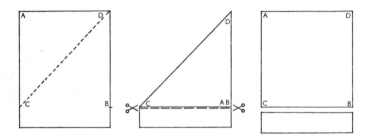

On the next two pages are shown the Origami symbols and what they mean. They are soon learned, and then you will be able to understand the drawings quite easily and be able to make the models perhaps even without reading the instructions on the facing pages. The written instructions are there in case you cannot quite follow the drawings.

The first two folds are the most important. They are the Valley Fold and the Mountain Fold. The drawings below help to explain them.

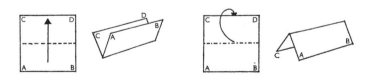

The Valley Fold is folded in front to make a trough. It is shown by a line of dashes.

The Mountain Fold is folded behind to make a ridge. It is shown by a line of dots and dashes.

Remember that if you pencil them on the paper, the dashes of the Valley Fold become hidden when you have made the fold, while the dots and dashes of the Mountain Fold remain visible.

The Symbols and their Meanings

Valley Fold

Mountain Fold

Cut

Existing crease

Fold in direction of arrow

Fold both sides behind in direction of arrows

Fold and tuck in

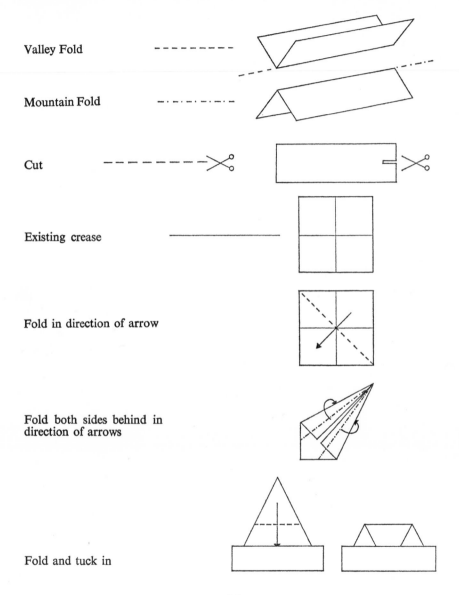

14

Blow at point indicated by arrow.

Repeat the fold shown on the front flap on similar flaps as many times as there are bars on the tail of arrow, leafing each flap over like the pages of a book. This is called Book Folding.

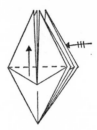

Fold over and over in direction of arrow.

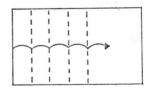

Turn model over in direction of arrow.

Hold here.

The drawings are numbered thus to correspond with the written instructions.

15

Reverse Folds

1. Take a rectangle of paper about six inches long and three inches wide and valley-fold this in half.
2. Valley-fold the doubled ends upwards in the direction of arrow.
3. The result should look like this. Bring the doubled ends down again. Mountain-fold on the same line. Bring the ends down again.
4. Push the creased ends up into the trough in the direction of arrow.
5. The Reverse Fold completed.

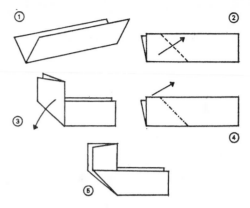

1. Make a crease in the doubled paper sloping in the opposite direction to Step 2 above, and work through Steps 2 to 4. This time bring the ends downwards so that the folds wrap round the trough.
5. The Wrap-around Reverse Fold completed.

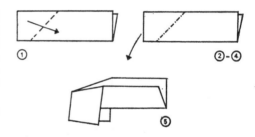

You can practise Reverse Folds with a triangular piece of paper to make a Swan's Neck.

1. Cut the folded rectangle from corner to corner.
2. Make the lower fold first. This will turn the neck inside out.
3. The base of the neck is reverse-folded. Now make the fold for the head.
4. The Swan's Neck completed.

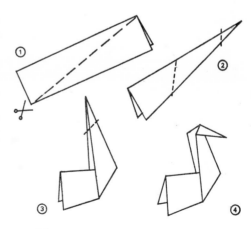

16

Crimp

1. Fold a rectangle of paper in half and make the two folds shown. Turn over and repeat the folds. Push the Valley Folds forward inside the Mountain Folds.

2. The Crimp completed. (This is another form of the Reverse Fold and can sometimes be used for making beaks, heads and so on.)

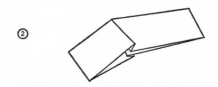

Rabbit's Ear

1. Fold down point A, making a light Valley Fold across the middle of the square. Open out.

2. Valley-fold AB on to the crease. Open out.

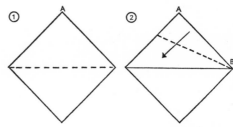

3. Valley-fold AC across in the same way. Open out.

4. Take hold of point A between finger and thumb and make the ear with a Valley Fold along AD and a Mountain Fold along DE.

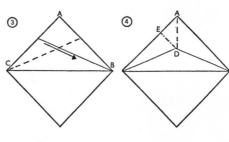

5. Push the ear over to the left and flatten.

6. The Rabbit's Ear completed.

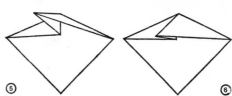

Handkerchief Base: Method 1

This is a simple way of making a series of folds which are used at the start of many models, and are also used for the Bird Base and the Frog Base.

1. Take a square of paper and valley-fold it across the middle both ways. Open out.
2. Mountain-fold across one diagonal, making the crease very sharp. Open out.
3. Bring the mountain-fold corners upright, points together. Bring the other two corners up so that all four corners meet. Then flatten the whole firmly.
4. The Handkerchief Base completed.

Water-bomb Base

This base is used to make the Squash and Petal Folds shown on the following pages.

1. Take a square of paper and valley-fold it across both diagonals. Open out.
2. Mountain-fold across the middle, making a very sharp crease. Open out.
3. Bring the mountain-fold uprights together. The four corners of the square will then come up of their own accord—two in front and two behind. Flatten firmly, and the Water-bomb Base is completed.

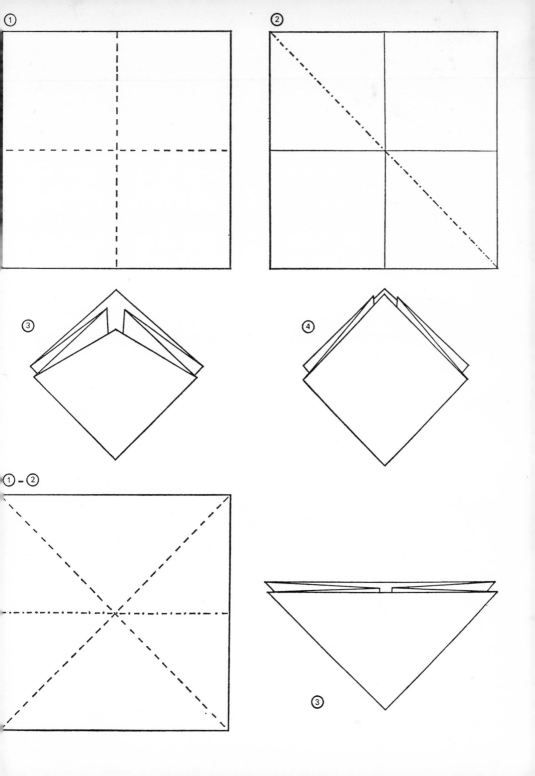

① ② ③ ④

① – ② ③

Squash Fold

Both the Squash Fold and the Petal Fold are used a great deal in making Bases and models.

1. Begin the Squash Fold with the Water-bomb Base, point upwards. Lift flap A and take it across so that AB lies along BC making a Valley Fold down the centre line BD. Lift up flap A and make a Mountain Fold along BE so that AB now lies along BD.
2. Lift up the whole of the folded flap and open its two edges at the bottom.
3. Place a finger inside. Lift up and flatten so that AB lies down the centre.
4. The Squash Fold completed.

Petal Fold

1. Begin with the Squash Fold. Lift point A. Make a Mountain Fold along DA. Repeat on the left along CA. Ignore the Valley Fold CD for the moment.
2. Lift up point A, opening the folds you have just made, and bring the two long edges together down the centre line. Press back along the Valley Fold CD so that point A lies on point B. Flatten.
3. The Petal Fold completed.

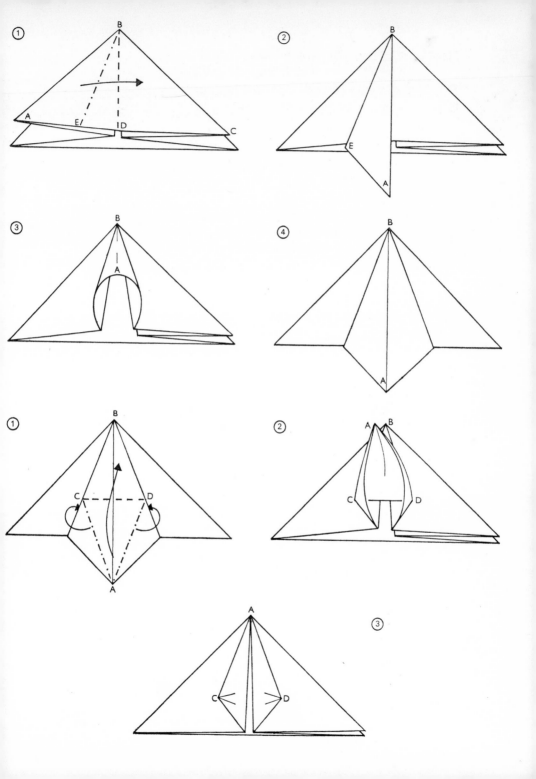

Handkerchief Base: Method 2

This time the Base is made with two Squash Folds.
1. Take a square of paper and fold it across one diagonal. Make a Valley Fold down the centre line BD.
2. Lift flap A and make a Mountain Fold along BE so that A goes to D.
3. Lift flap A right over so that we are back at Step 1. Open up the edges on the left and make a Squash Fold so that A comes down on to point D.
4. The first Squash Fold is now completed. Make a Mountain Fold along BF, taking point C to the back. Turn over. Lift flap C right back and make the second Squash Fold like the first.
5. The Handkerchief Base (Method 2) completed.

In Method 1 (page 18) both square faces are plain. Method 2 has a crease line down the centre which provides a useful guide-line for some of the models.

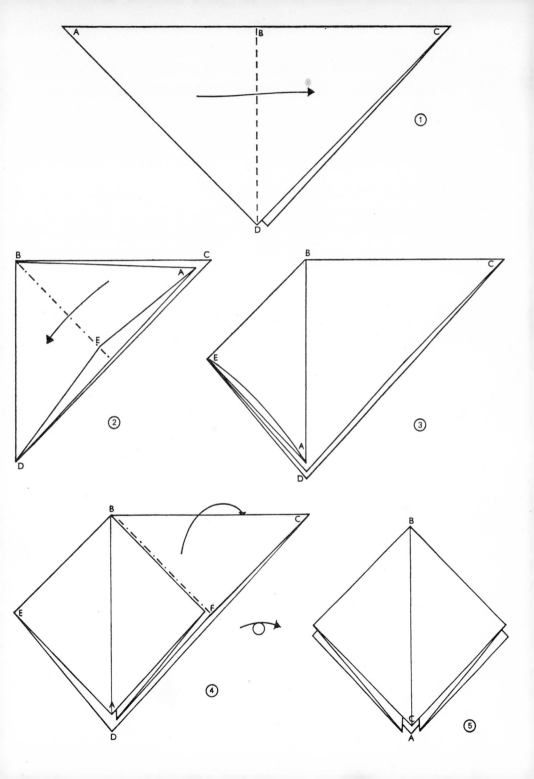

Envelope Base

1. Take a square of paper and fold it in half both ways. Open out. Valley-fold the four corners to the centre of the square. Press flat and crease the edges well. See that the outer corners of the new and smaller square are sharp and neat.
2. The Envelope Base completed.

If you have followed the directions carefully so far you should now be able to make all the models in Sections 2 and 3.

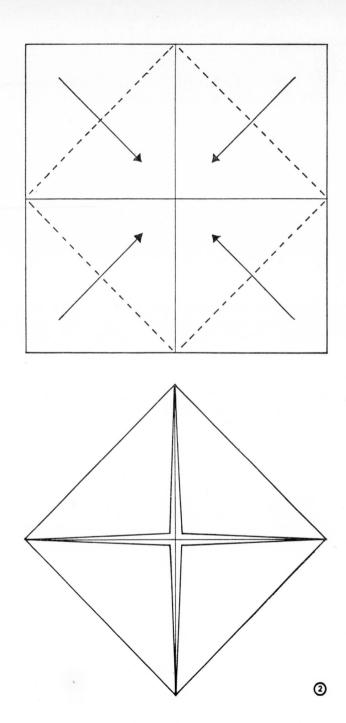

Diamond Base

1. Take a square of paper. If you are using coloured paper, place the coloured surface downwards and the uncoloured one towards you. Make a Valley Fold down the diagonal AB. Open out. Make Valley Folds on both sides where shown so that the two top edges of the square lie along line AB.
2. Make two Valley Folds where shown so that the bottom edges of the flaps lie along the centre line AB.
3. The Diamond Base completed. This is used to make the Fish Base and the models on pages 58 to 61.

Fish Base

3. Begin with the Diamond Base. Make a Valley Fold where shown, taking point A down to point B. In other words, fold the Diamond Base in half. Open out. Hold down the Valley Fold with a finger of the left hand. With the other hand pull up the corner hidden behind flap C to the centre line. Flatten flap C to make a Rabbit's Ear (see page 17). Repeat on the other side with flap D.
4. The Rabbit's Ears completed. This is the first position of the Fish Base. Now fold flap A down behind to touch B.
5. The Fish Base completed in its second position. Note the resemblance to the mouth of a fish.

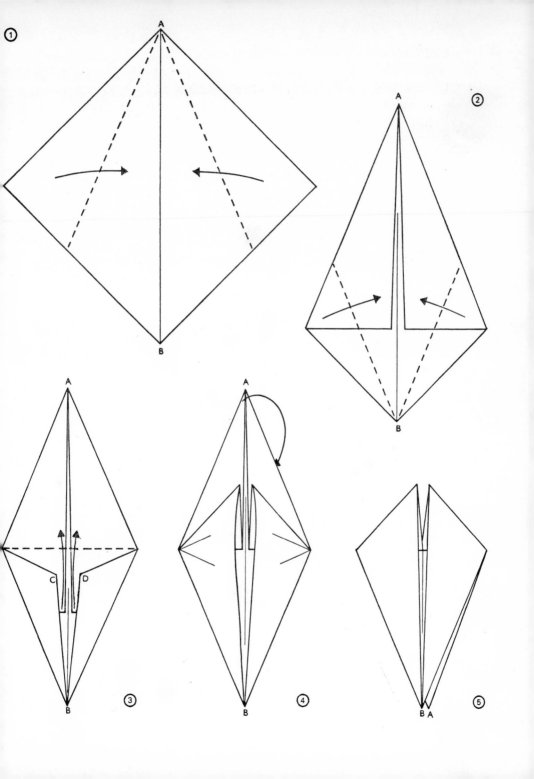

Bird Base

1. Begin with the Handkerchief Base (Method 1), its open ends downwards. Ignore the Valley Fold for the moment but make the two Mountain Folds with the side flaps. Repeat at the back.
2. Make the Valley Fold shown. Lift the flap and open up the four Mountain Folds you first made.
3. Lift point A right up. The two side flaps will lift and the two long edges should come together. Flatten to make a Petal Fold in front (see pages 20 and 21).
4. The front Petal Fold completed. Turn over and repeat Steps 2 and 3 on the back.
5. Valley-fold point A down to the bottom. Turn over. Repeat with the flap at the back.
6. The Bird Base completed.

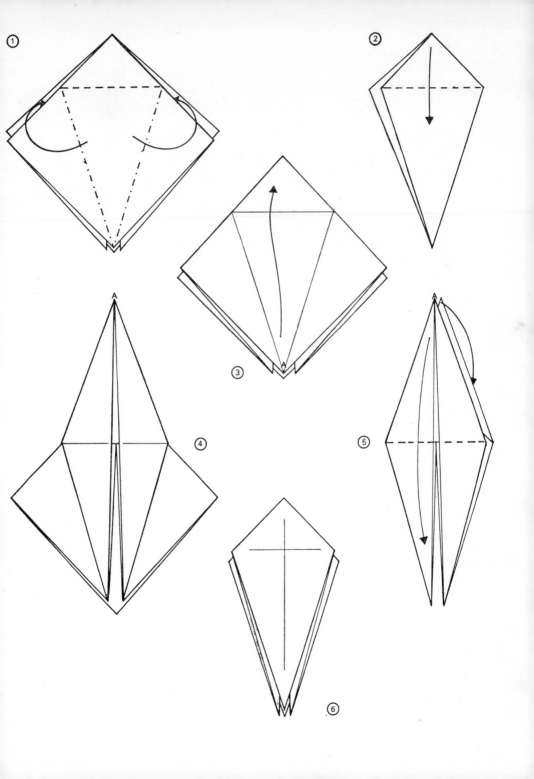

Frog Base

1. Begin with the Handkerchief Base (Method 2), open ends downwards. Make the Valley and Mountain Folds shown and squash-fold the flap.
2. Mountain-fold the two side flaps of the Squash Fold. Open out.
3. Lift up the edge between the two side flaps and make a Petal Fold.
4. The Petal Fold completed. Repeat Steps 1 to 3 on all the three other flaps, leafing over like the pages of a book to find the blank faces. It does not matter which way you turn the leaves but you must finish with four flaps on the left and four on the right.
5. The Frog Base completed.

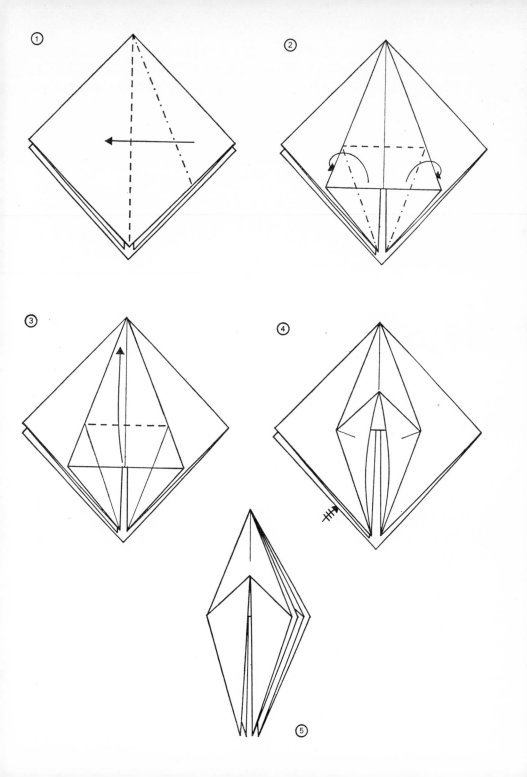

Simple Models Made Without Bases

Chinese Knight's Helmet

1. Take a square of paper and fold it across one diagonal. Valley-fold A and B to the bottom point.
2. Valley-fold flaps A and B upwards.
3. Valley-fold flaps A and B outwards so that AB lies parallel with CD (see Diagram 4).
4. Valley-fold the top layer from the bottom point where shown.
5. Valley-fold the same flap along CD. Turn over.
6. Valley-fold points C and D towards the centre.
7. Valley-fold the bottom flap upwards where shown. Turn over.
8. Open the hat along the bottom.
9. The Chinese Knight's Helmet completed.

The helmet can be made from paper coloured on one side, or from two squares of differently coloured papers laid one on top of the other. It will fit a small head if it is made from a square with sides about 22 inches long.

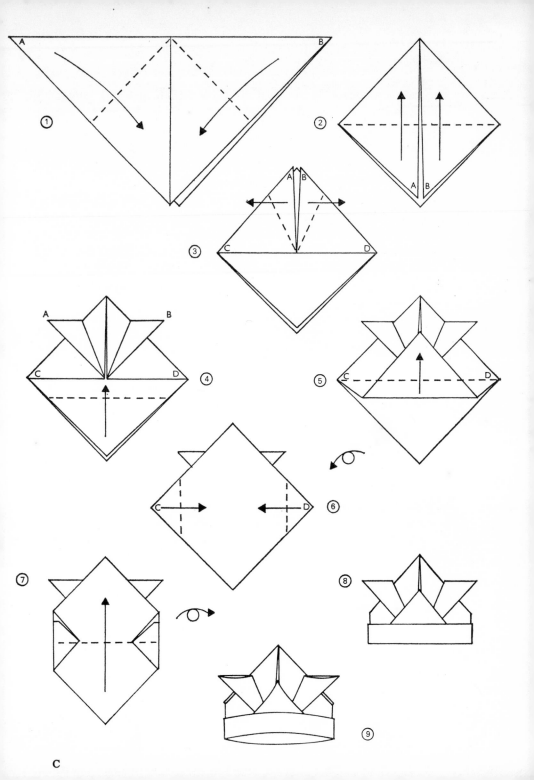

C

Rabbit

1. Take a square of paper. Valley-fold it in half and then across both diagonals. Open out flat.
2. Valley-fold sides AC and BD to the centre line.
3. Valley-fold the top edge down to the centre point X.
4. Points A and B are now underneath. Pull them upwards and outwards. Flatten along the diagonal creases made in Step 1.
5. Valley-fold the top corners over on lines AE and EB. Mountain-fold the bottom corners behind on the diagonal guide lines.
6. Mountain-fold the whole model in half.
7. Make a Reverse Fold for the tail (see page 16). Bend the rabbit's head on the marks of the Valley Fold so that the model will stand up.
8. The Rabbit completed. You can make a family of babies as shown in the drawing.

Sailing Boat

1. Take a square of paper and fold it along one diagonal. Make a Reverse Fold to form the hull (see page 16).
2. Mountain-fold all the thicknesses together at the bottom. If you make the crease very sharp the boat will stand.
3. The Sailing Boat completed.

The height of the sail and the depth of the hull can be varied by changing the angle of the Reverse Fold in Step 1.

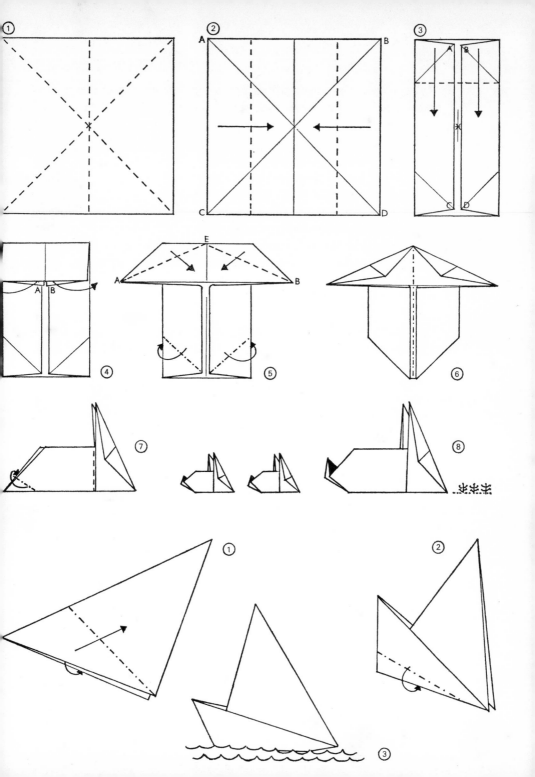

Cicada

1. Take a square of paper coloured on one side, coloured side downwards. Fold it along one diagonal. Make two Valley Folds, taking points A and B up to meet point C.
2. Valley-fold A and B down again at a slight angle so that the wing-tips come below the tail of the cicada.
3. Valley-fold flap C downwards, one layer only.
4. Valley-fold the other layer, flap D, downwards.
5. Mountain-fold both sides. Turn over. EF and GH should lie close to the centre line at the back.
6. Mountain-fold the two top corners to make the eyes. Valley-fold lightly down the centre line of the insect and open up again. Turn over.
7. The Cicada completed.

The cicada is a large, winged beetle found in both tropical and subtropical countries—even sometimes in the south of England. It makes a shrill, rasping noise with two drum-like sounding boards on each side of its stomach. The warmer the sun is the louder is its cry, which is believed to be a mating call.

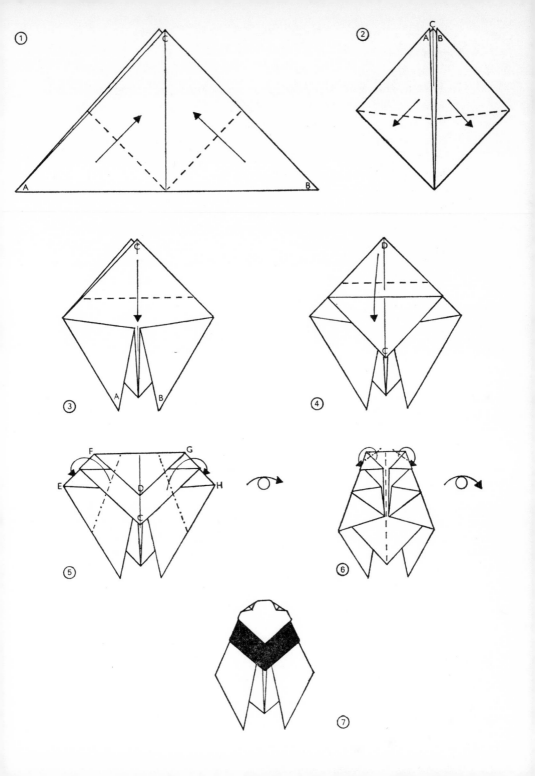

Pigeon

1. Take a square of paper coloured on one side, coloured side downwards. Fold it along one diagonal, points at the bottom. Valley-fold the centre line so that B falls on C. Open out. Mountain-fold along line DE, which is about one-third of the way down the triangle.
2. Valley-fold point A upwards, one layer only. This fold should come half-way between the lines BC and DE.
3. Valley-fold the model in half down the centre line, taking EC across to DB. Turn it to the position shown in Step 4.
4. Reverse-fold the head at A (see page 16). Valley-fold the top wing upwards, lifting at point C.
5. The top wing is now up. Valley-fold point C down where shown. Turn over and repeat Steps 4 and 5 on the other wing. Mark in the eyes with pencil or ink.
6. The Pigeon completed.

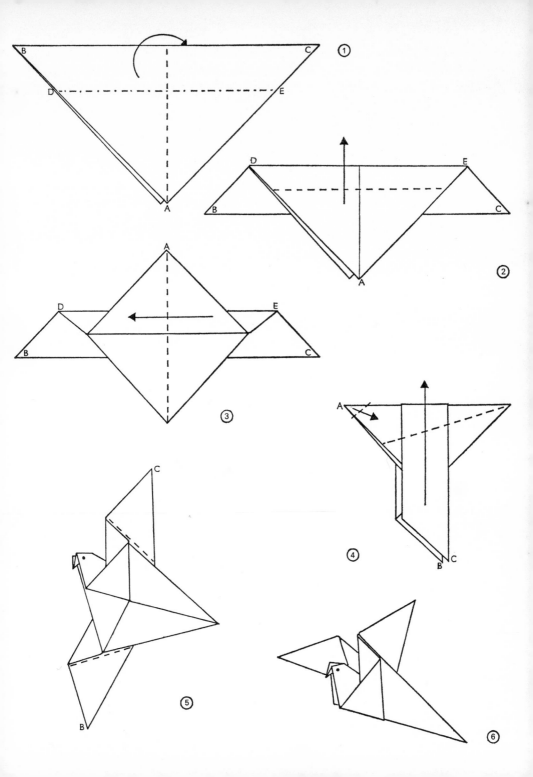

Elephant

Brown or black paper is good for this model.
1. Take a square of paper and valley-fold it along one diagonal. Open out. Valley-fold the two sides to the crease line.
2. Valley-fold along the diagonal.
3. Make the Valley Fold along BE so that AB lies parallel with CD.
4. Valley-fold so that EA lies along EB. Lift up. Open up the edges and make a Squash Fold (see pages 20 and 21). EA should again lie along EB.
5. Mountain-fold the head along its centre line so that it wraps round the body. Make a firm crease.
6. Reverse-fold the trunk (see page 16). Cut away the shaded parts to make the legs and tail. Mark in the eyes with pen or pencil, or stamp them out with a small paper-punch.
7. The Elephant completed.

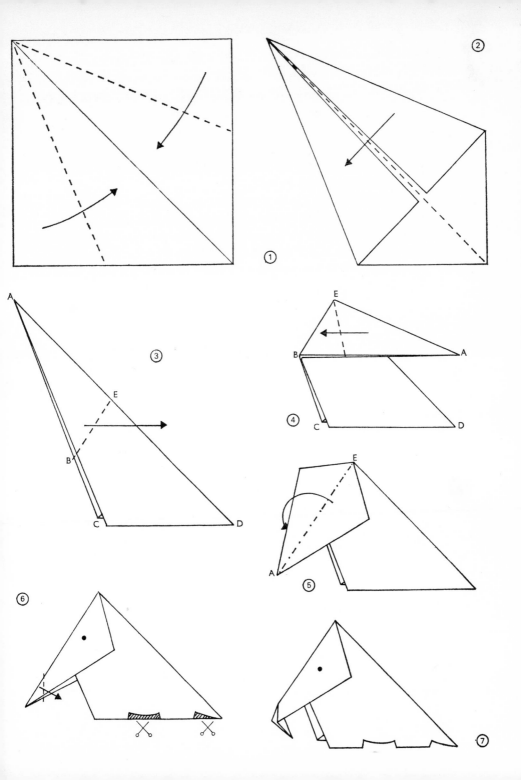

Swan

1. Take a square of white paper. Valley-fold along one diagonal. Open out. Valley-fold the two sides to the centre.
2. Mountain-fold both side flaps to the centre line at the back. You may find it easier to turn the model over and valley-fold the flaps, but then you must turn it back again for Step 3.
3. Valley-fold the model in half.
4. Make two Reverse Folds where shown (see page 16). Start with the lower one, making a Valley Fold along the line before making the Reverse Fold.
5. This shows the model with only the lower Reverse Fold completed. Now complete the upper Reverse Fold to make the beak and head.
6. The Swan completed.

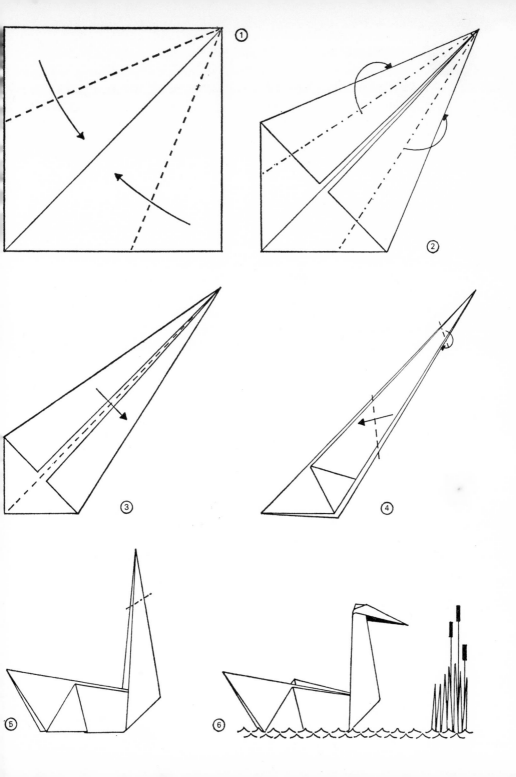

Japanese Woman

1. Take a square of paper either coloured or, better, having a pattern on one side. Place the plain side upwards. Crease across one diagonal and open out. Valley-fold both sides to the diagonal.
2. Mountain-fold about one-third of the way down the diagonal, making a firm crease line. Open out.
3. Mountain-fold three-quarters of the way down the top triangle which was formed in Step 2. Turn over.
4. Pencil in and cut away the shaded areas at the neck. Mark dots with a pencil at the two inner corners of the neck triangles you have just cut out. Lift the head and cut a slot between the two pencil marks.
5. Make a Valley Fold and pass the head through the slot.
6. Cut along the sides of the dress and then cut the top layer of paper only along each side nearly up to the neck-slot.
7. Valley-fold so that the head comes up from behind.
8. Valley-fold the top layers of both side flaps to the centre line. Lift the yoke of the dress as you do this and tuck the flaps underneath it.
9. Valley-fold the remaining two side flaps from the shoulder downwards. Then valley-fold the tip of the head and tuck it into the neck-slot.
10. This drawing and the next are enlarged. Make the Mountain Folds shown.
11. The Japanese Woman completed.

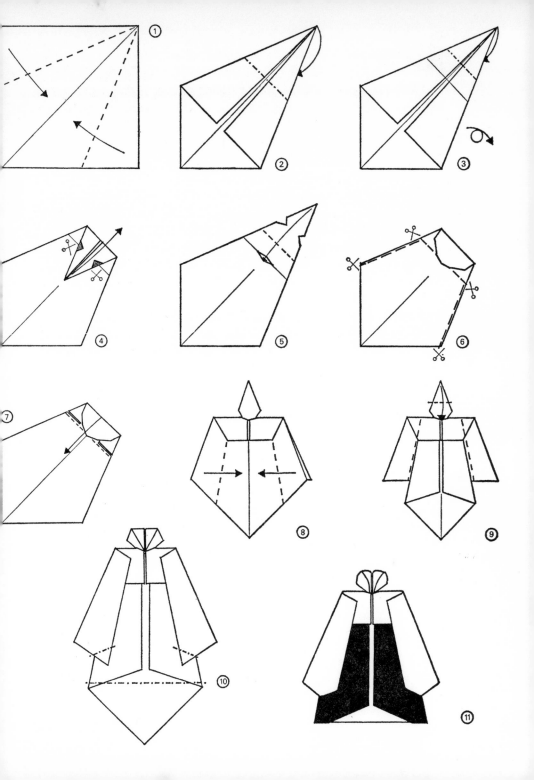

Japanese Man

1. Take a square of paper coloured, or patterned, on one side, plain side upwards. Crease in half both ways and along both diagonals. Open out. Make the four cuts shown, each cut being a little less than half-way to the centre-point of the square. Mountain-fold the two flaps formed by the cuts.
2. Valley-fold the pointed flap down.
3. Pencil in and cut the shaded area at the neck. Mark with the pencil the inner corners of the neck triangles. Lift the head and cut a slot between the two pencil marks.
4. Pass the head through the neck-slot. Now make the Valley Fold shown on the right, taking the whole side flap across the body. Mountain-fold this flap back where shown, so forming a pleat. Repeat on the left side.
5. Valley-fold down so that the head comes up from behind.
6. Hold the model on the right shoulder between thumb and finger and pull the sleeve upwards, so undoing the pleat up to the shoulder point. Crease flat. Repeat on the left shoulder. Make the Valley Folds at the waist to form the belt.
7. Valley-fold the skirt upwards, tucking the point under the yoke. Make the Valley and Mountain Folds shown on the head and hands.
8. Valley-fold the arms downwards, making a light crease except near the shoulder. This will give a slight curve to the sleeves.
9. The Japanese Man completed.

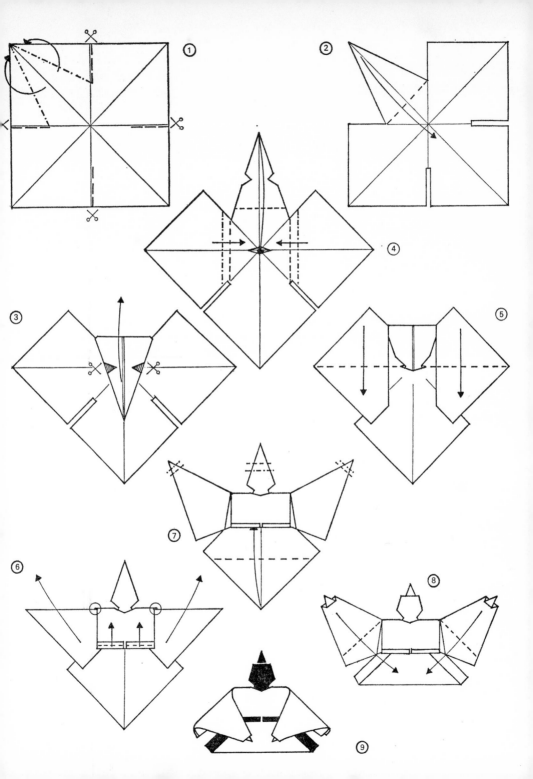

3

Models Made from the Envelope Base

Salt Cellar

1. Take a square of paper and make the Envelope Base (see pages 24 and 25). Turn over.
2. Valley-fold all four corners to the centre. Turn over.
3. Mountain-fold between the four square flaps. Mountain-fold lightly across the two diagonals of the whole square.
4. Lift the four flaps and place a thumb and three fingers of the right hand into the four pockets. At the same time push up the centre-point from behind with a finger of the left hand. As the pockets open, remove your left hand, grip the model with your right hand and bring the bottom points of the salt cellar together like pincers. Release your fingers and it will stand.
5. The Salt Cellar completed.

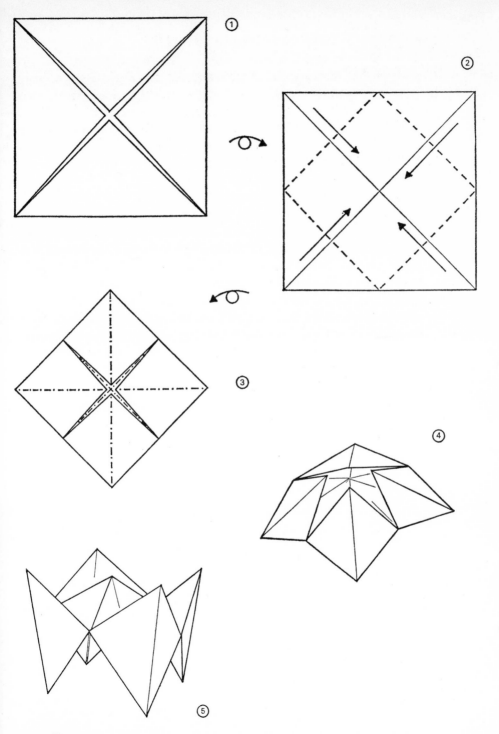

D

Lotus Flower

Use paper that is strong but pliable and not too thick. Take a fairly large square, because the series of folds reduces the paper quickly to a small size. A seven-inch square will do well. Make all creases very sharp.

1. Begin with the Envelope Base. Valley-fold all four corners to the centre.
2. Valley-fold the corners again to the centre.
3. The model should now look like this. Turn over.
4. Once more valley-fold the corners to the centre.
5. Now begin to form the petals. First lift one corner of the square, bending the flap at the valley-fold line. Then pull up the corner flap rising up behind gently but firmly over the first corner as far as it will go, while pressing the first corner beneath it down and back. Repeat at the other three corners to complete the first four petals.
6. This is an enlarged view showing these petals being formed. Now pull up four more corner flaps in turn from the back, working them right up and over as far as they will come but without tearing the paper. Finally pull the four single corner flaps from the bottom up and over in the same way.
7. The Lotus Flower completed.

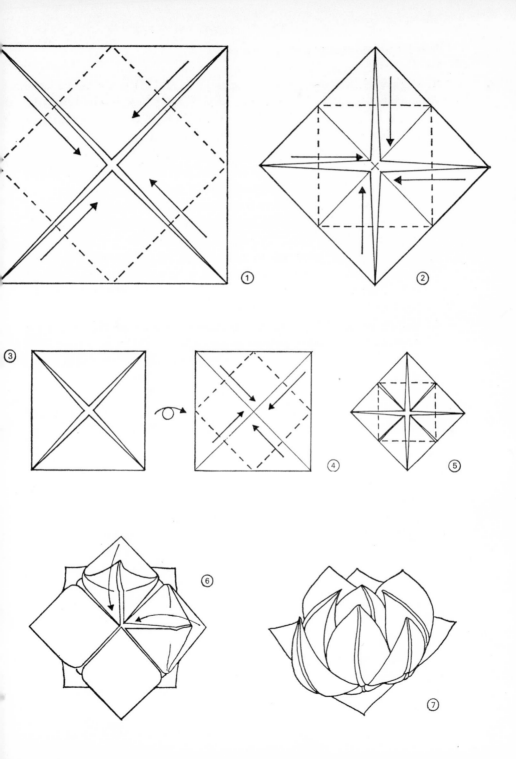

Four-legged Container and Carpenter's Hat

1. Begin with the Envelope Base (see pages 24 and 25), again using a large square. Mountain-fold the Envelope Base in half, points upwards.
2. Make a Mountain Fold and then a Valley Fold where shown. Open out. Put a finger between the doubled edges ABC and make a Squash Fold in front so that point A falls on C at the top and B falls on D.
3. Repeat the steps in 2 making the Squash Fold at the back. You will now have made a Handkerchief Base of double thickness.
4. Valley-fold point A down to E. Lift it up again. Put a finger between the edges of AE, pull up the edges and make a Squash Fold so that A falls on E and the square becomes a rectangle.
5. Valley-fold the rectangle in half. Open out. Valley-fold the two bottom corners. Open them out. Put a finger between the bottom layers, lift up and then squash-fold both ends of the rectangle to produce Figure 6. Turn over and repeat Steps 4 and 5 at the back.
6. Valley-fold the whole top layer on the left over to the right so that a plain surface appears. Repeat at the back.
7. Valley-fold the single corner flaps where shown in front and at back.
8. Valley-fold the sides to the centre in front and at back.
9. Make the two Valley Folds, the top one first. Repeat at the back.
10. Tuck the corners of the flap into the two pockets. Repeat at back.
11. Open out and stand. The Container completed.

The Carpenter's Hat is made by turning the container upside down and tucking in all the leg points. If you leave up one of the flaps made in Step 10 and do not tuck it in, you will have a Japanese Soldier's Hat.

12. The Carpenter's Hat completed.

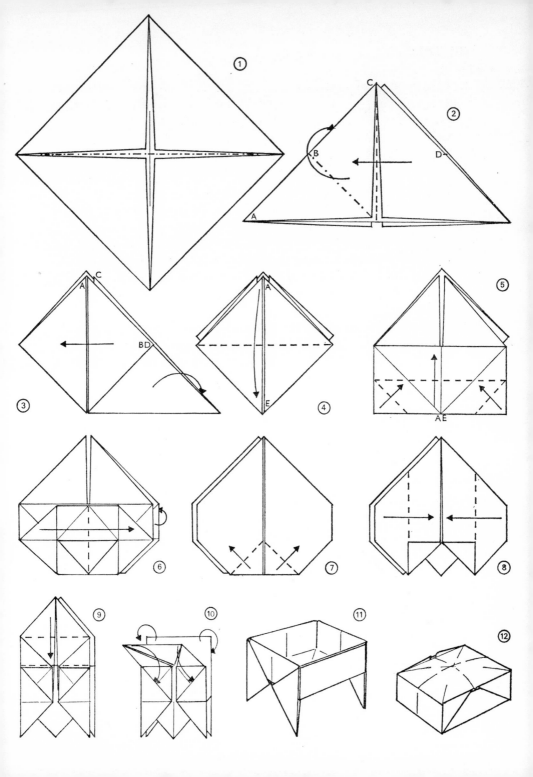

Gift Box

1. Take a square of paper, the stiffer the better. If coloured or patterned, fold with the plain side upwards. Crease both diagonals and fold in half both ways. Valley-fold two corners to the centre.
2. Valley-fold the sides to the centre line, making sharp creases.
3. Valley-fold top and bottom points to the centre.
4. Valley-fold top and bottom edges to the centre.
5. Open out the whole square. Now all the guide lines show as creases.
6. Cut away the shaded areas and pencil in the heavily marked central square which will form the bottom of the box.
7. Mark in all the letters shown and also the slits and slots. Cut the four slits marked X up to the points A,B,C and D of the central square. Cut the slits on each side of the flaps F,H,I and K. Cut slots in the middle of flaps E,G,J and L. The slots and slits are shown as double lines for clarity but only single cuts are needed.
8. Bend up the sides along the edges of the square ABCD, creasing well. Pass flap F through slot E. Fold the edges of the flap lightly towards each other as you pass the flap through the slot and then open them out. Pass flap H through slot G. Bring the large flap I across and pass it through slot J. Finally pass flap K through slot L.
9. The Gift Box completed.

The box looks charming if made with a paper covered with a small but gaily coloured pattern like that obtainable for book ends. Any size of box can be made to fit any kind of gift. You can make a nest of several boxes, one fitting into the other, with a precious gift inside the smallest box.

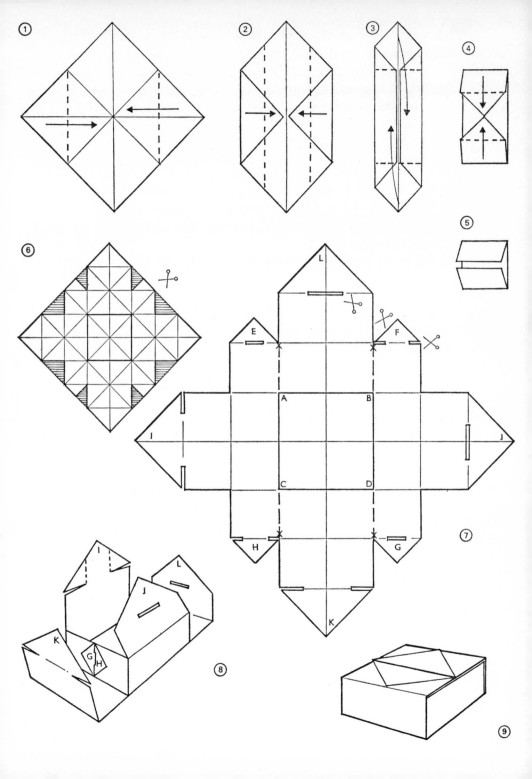

Fishing Boat

1. Take a square of coloured paper, coloured side downwards. The paper should be thin and pliable. Fold in half both ways and then across both diagonals. Open out. Make the Envelope Base (see pages 24 and 25), but with the points slightly away from the centre. A small square may be drawn in the centre so that the distances of the points from the centre are all equal. Turn over.
2. Valley-fold both sides to the centre.
3. Valley-fold the four corners along the lines shown.
4. Make the four Valley Folds shown. The folds will lie better if you just miss the centre line.
5. Make the two Valley Folds shown so that the points touch at the centre.
6. Mountain-fold the model in half.
7. This is a view looking down on to the bottom of the boat, where three long folded layers run down the centre. Take hold of the layers on each side of the centre fold, index fingers inside and thumbs outside. Turn the boat inside out. This is easier to do than it sounds, but be careful not to undo any of the folds. Pull slightly outwards as you turn.
8. The Fishing Boat completed. If you lift the pointed flaps at each end you will have protection for wet and stormy weather. Or you can have only one hood up for protection against waves at the bow of the boat.
9. The Fishing Boat completed with both flaps up. If made with waxed paper it will last a long time in the water.

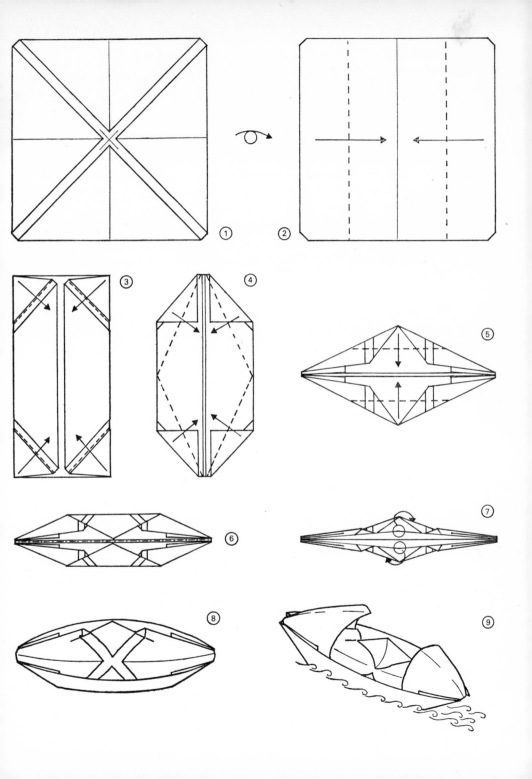

4

Models Made from the Diamond Base and the Fish Base

Mouse

1. Begin with the Diamond Base (see pages 26 and 27). Valley-fold point A down in the direction of B as in Diagram 2, making sure that the folding line is just above the middle.
2. Lift up point A and unfold the Diamond Base. Fold the square along diagonal AB.
3. Cut through both layers of paper from A to X to make the tail. Re-fold the Diamond Base on the existing crease lines and lay it flat on the table.
4. and 5. Lift points C and D and valley-fold the flaps where shown so that the flaps cross each other on the centre line. Mark the positions of the ear slots. Lift back C and D. Fold the model in half and cut the slots for the ears right through all the layers of paper with sharply pointed scissors. Open the model. Draw in the whisker lines and cut carefully from the centre outwards through the single layers of paper towards the folded edges, being careful not to cut too far on to the end of the nose. Diagram 5 gives an enlarged view of all the cuts. Cross flaps C and D again and pass their points through the two ear slits. Valley-fold the whiskers towards the nose.
6. Valley-fold the model in half and crease well.
7. This is an enlarged view of the head after the model has been folded in half. Open up the ears with the tip of a pencil or scissors and squash flat on the Valley Fold line. Valley-fold the whiskers upwards.
8. This is an enlarged view of the ears and whiskers in position. Add the eyes with a pen, pencil or crayon. Red eyes on a white mouse look right.
9. The Mouse completed.

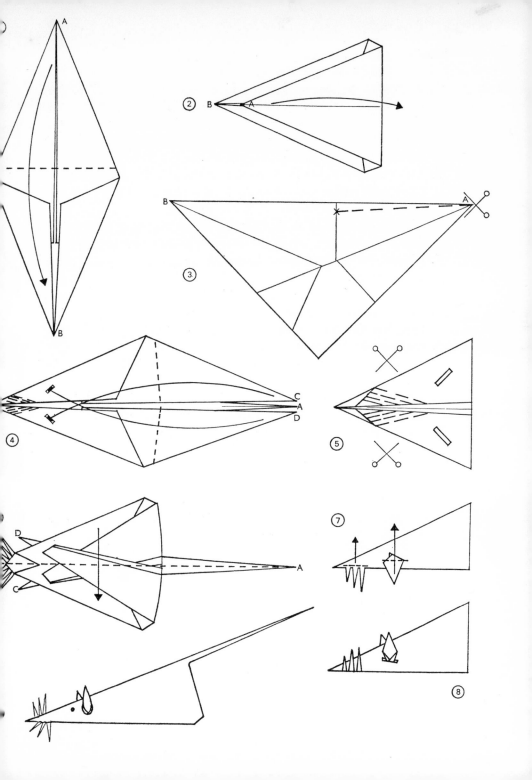

Mask

1. Begin with the Diamond Base folded to Step 1 on page 27. Make the two Valley Folds and the two Mountain Folds shown. (The top Valley Fold must always be in the same position whenever you make a mask, but the positions of the other folds can be changed to vary the final expression of the face.)
2. Make the two Valley Folds on the top flap, the lower one first. Tuck tip B underneath. Make a Valley Fold on the lower flap to make the nose, and tuck in tip A.
3. Make a Valley Fold on the chin and then a Mountain Fold below it. Do this so that the top of the nose will remain tucked in.
4. Mountain-fold the sides of the mouth and chin. Valley-fold the hair on each side.
5. Mountain-fold the right side. Hold the cheek with one hand and lift the top corner. Squash this into a Rabbit's Ear (see page 17) to form the side-piece of the hair. Repeat on the left side.
6. Make the Mountain Folds shown.
7. Mountain-fold the sides and centre line slightly. Make the eye folds as follows.
8. and 9. These are enlarged views of one eye, showing the folds. Lift the loose end and make a Squash Fold towards the nose. Lift up the fold and make the Mountain Fold if you want slanting hooded eyes.
10. The Mask completed. If you want to make a life-size mask to wear, you must start with a square of paper with sides about 14 inches long. When you have made one, punch a hole on each side close to the eye and attach a piece of string or elastic to the mask through the holes to pull over your head.

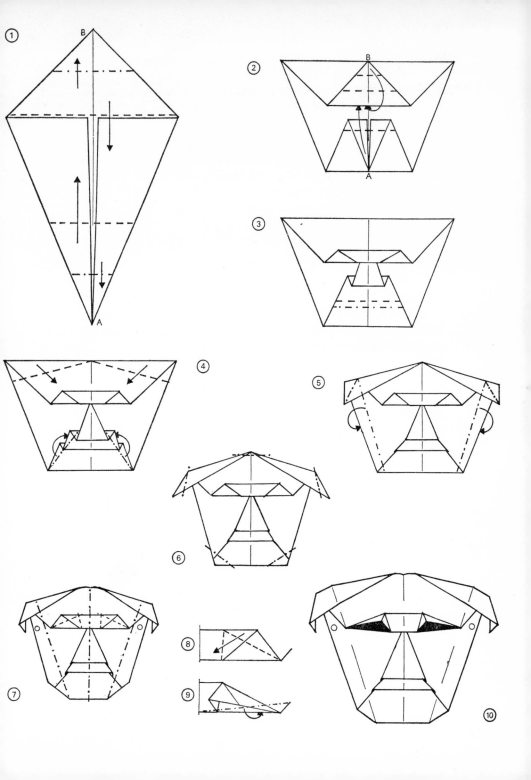

Whale

1. Begin with the first position of the Fish Base but with the flaps down (see pages 26 and 27), preferably using black paper. Mountain-fold the model in half down the centre.
2. Valley-fold the fin. Repeat behind on the other fin.
3. Reverse-fold the head so that point A disappears into the body of the whale. Reverse-fold the tail. (See page 16 if in doubt about reverse-folds.)
4. The Whale completed.

Angel Fish

1. Begin with the Fish Base as in Diagram 1 of the Whale. Valley-fold in half so that the flaps are inside. Make the two reverse-folds at a slight angle which will let points A and B overlap when the folds have been made as in Diagram 2.
2. Reverse-fold points A and B for the tail. Lift the top flap of the head at point C. Take hold of E and pass it right across the body between the two head flaps to form the other fin. Press flat. Pencil or ink small circles for the two eyes.
3. The Angel Fish completed. It looks very pretty if made with red paper.

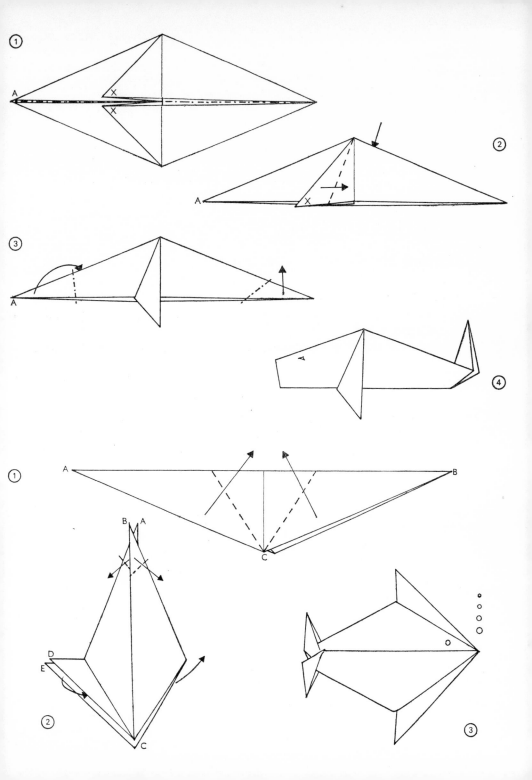

5

Models Made from the Bird Base

Flapping Bird

1. Begin with the Bird Base (see pages 28 and 29). Take point A to the top. Repeat at the back. Now you have the two divided points at the bottom.
2. Fold the front flap on the left over to the right so that B comes to C. Repeat at the back.
3. Now two divided points are at the top. Valley-fold the bottom point up to the top (lifting the top leaf only). Repeat at the back.
4. Hold the model firmly at the centre with the left hand and take hold of the inner point on the right with your right hand. Pull outwards and downwards to make the tail. Change hands and repeat with the left flap to make the head. Crease firmly. The correct angles are shown in the next drawing.
5. Reverse-fold to make the head and beak. If you hold the base of the neck between thumb and finger of one hand and pull the tail with the other hand, the bird will flap its wings.
6. The Flapping Bird completed.

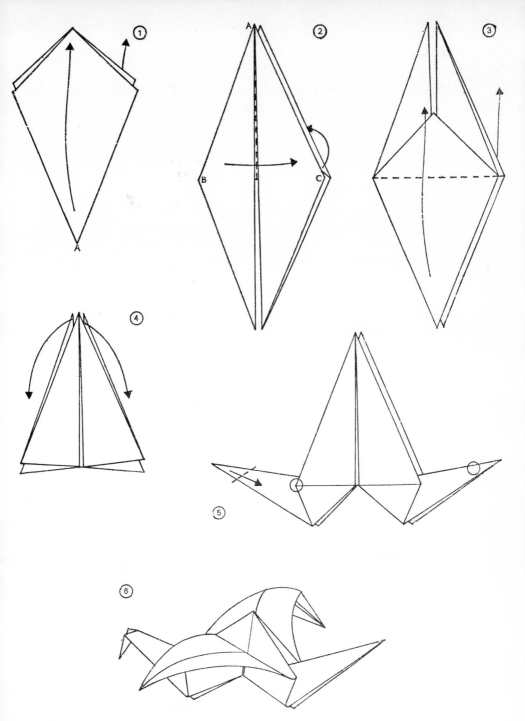

E

Crane

1. Begin with the Bird Base (see pages 28 and 29). Take the points to the top as you did with the Flapping Bird.
2. Valley-fold the two sides to the centre. Repeat at the back. Make very sharp points for the delicate beak and tail.
3. Make the two Reverse Folds shown, taking the points up between the wings.
4. Reverse-fold the head.
5. Pull the head and tail down slightly and then take hold of the two wings. Pull them gently in opposite directions to open out the body. Blow into the hole at the bottom marked by the arrow until the body is fully inflated. Curl the wings round a pencil.
6. The Crane completed.

The Japanese call the Crane a lucky bird, and it is the most popular of all Origami models in Japan.

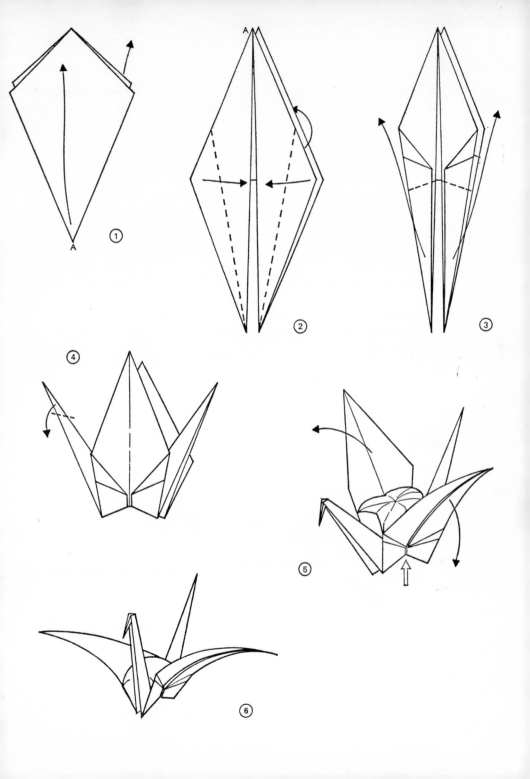

Turtle

1. Begin with the Bird Base and fold as in Step 1 of the Flapping Bird (page 64). Turn upside down so that the divided points are at the top. Make the Mountain Fold and the two Valley Folds on the front flap only, starting with the top Valley Fold.
2. Valley-fold the flap upwards. Make the two Mountain Folds for the front legs, so that the shoulders come just above the back. (You may find it easier to lift the head flap back again while you do this.)
3. Reverse-fold the Mountain Folds of the two legs you have just made.
4. The model should now look like this. Turn over.
5. Lift up the bottom flap and make the Valley Fold and then the Mountain Fold.
6. Cut up the centre line of the bottom flap. Make a Valley Fold on each side to form the two back legs.
7. The model should look like this. Turn over.
8. The Turtle completed. The layers will hold together well and the turtle will stand on its four legs if you mountain-fold the body down the centre. Make the crease lightly.

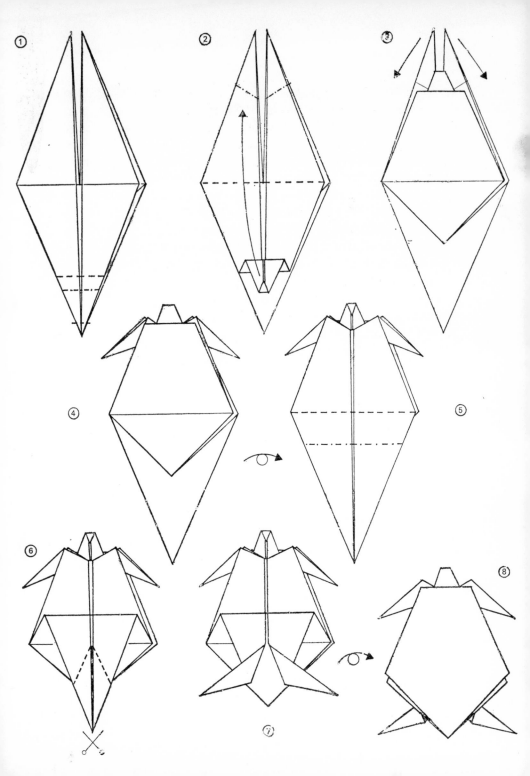

Owl

1. Begin with the Bird Base (see pages 28 and 29). Valley-fold the two top flaps to the centre. Repeat at the back.
2. Take hold of the point at the bottom on the left which lies below the top flap, and pull it upwards and outwards. Then twist it so that the divided face is towards you and squash it flat to make one wing. Repeat with the right point to make the other wing.
3. Make the top Valley Fold, then the Mountain Fold and finally the Valley Fold down again to form the beak and head.
4. The model should now look like this. Turn over.
5. Lift up the head at the back and make the two cuts, taking care to cut through the back of the head only. Bend up the cut pieces to form the ears. Turn over.
6. Cut along the centre line of the upper layer at the tail and valley-fold the two pieces upwards to make the feet.
7. The Owl completed.

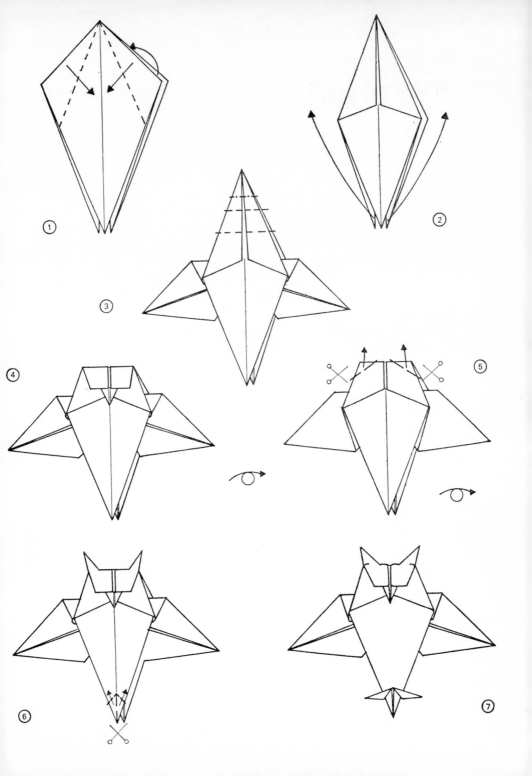

Dragonfly

1. Begin with the Bird Base (see pages 28 and 29, folded as far as Diagram 5). Fold down the flap at the back to the bottom.
2. Valley-fold the right-hand point in the direction of the arrow. Bring it down again. Lift it upwards and outwards, as you did with the owl's wings, taking up point B to lie under point C while twisting and opening the flap to the front so that the divided face shows and making a Mountain Fold along AD. Repeat on the left.
3. The model should look like this. Starting at the top, make the Valley Fold on the right, taking D across to A and pulling point BC over to make a Squash Fold along the line ending at E. Repeat on the left.
4. The model should now look like this. Turn over.
5. Make Valley Folds and Squash Folds on both sides as in Step 3.
6. Mountain-fold the model in half.
7. Reverse-fold where shown.
8. Turn the dragonfly on its back and valley-fold the flap over and over to make the head as shown in the lower drawing, finally wrapping the whole around the neck and squashing it. Cut the two wings from the top down to the body.
9. Valley-fold the four wing-tips. Valley-fold both wings along the body line.
10. The Dragonfly completed.

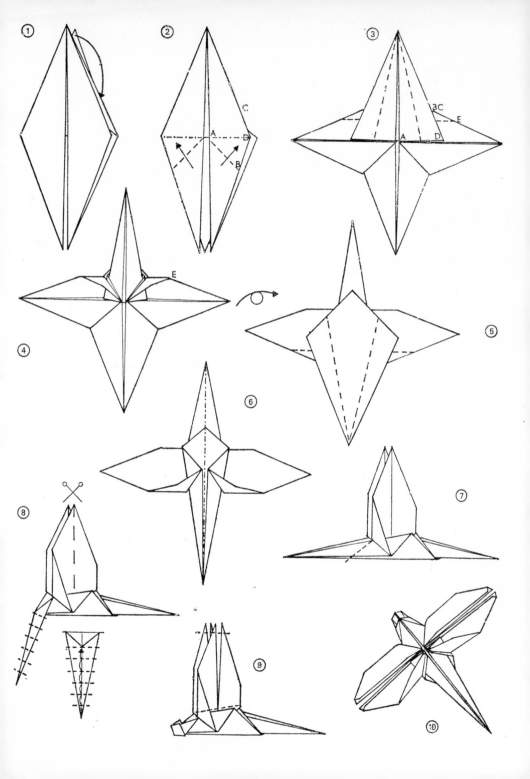

6

Models Made from the Frog Base

Jumping Frog

1. Take a square of green paper and make the Frog Base (see pages 30 and 31). Book-fold in front and at the back so that plain faces show.
2. Valley-fold the front flaps to the centre line. Repeat at the back and on the other two plain faces you will find by leafing over.
3. The model should look like this. Book-fold in front and at the back as in Step 1.
4. Reverse-fold the two front flaps to the angles shown to form the front legs.
5. Now the model should look like this. Turn over.
6. Reverse-fold the remaining two flaps to form the back legs.
7. Reverse-fold all four legs. Turn over.
8. Reverse-fold all four legs again unless the model is very small, when simple folds will do. Hold the model where shown and blow hard into the body where the arrow indicates. Turn over.
9. The Jumping Frog completed. If you stroke the frog's back gently with your finger so that the finger slips sharply on to the table, he will jump.

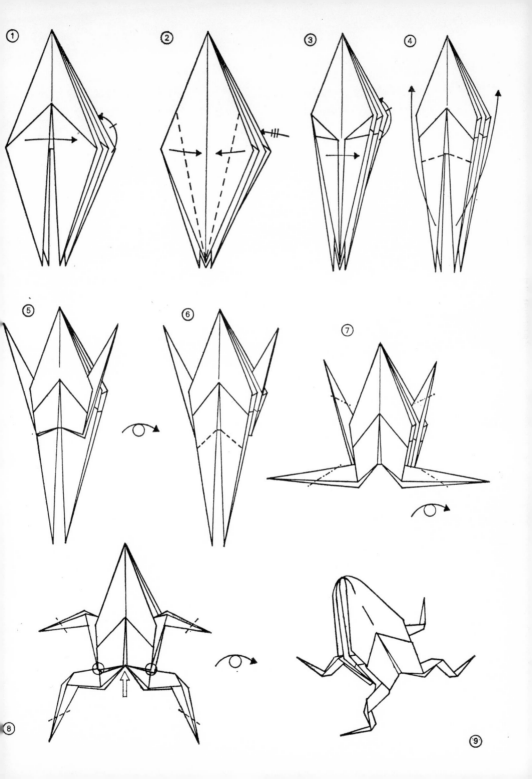

Octopus

1. Begin with the Frog Base and fold Steps 1 and 2 of the Jumping Frog on the two previous pages.
2. Valley-fold the front flap up. Repeat at the back and on the two remaining faces you will find by leafing over.
3. The model should look like this. Stand it up. Hold the centre pyramid and carefully flatten the points on the table.
4. Cut each of the four flattened flaps along to the fold lines to make eight tentacles. Make a fold across every other tentacle close to the body to prevent the tentacles' crossing one another. Or fold them as you like. Blow up the body from underneath as hard as you can.
5. The Octopus completed.

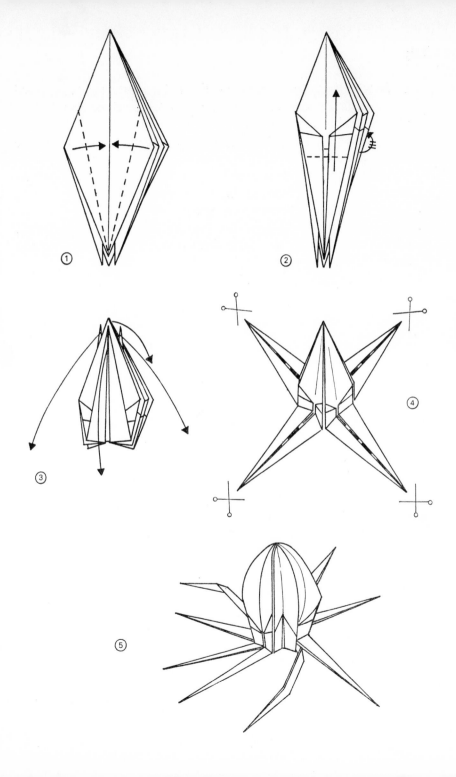

Lily

1. Begin with the Frog Base, the divided points at the top. Valley-fold the small flap upwards. Repeat at the back and on the other two faces you will find by leafing over.
2. Valley-fold in front and at the back so that you have a plain face back and front.
3. Valley-fold the side flaps to the centre. Repeat at the back and on the other two plain faces, leafing as before to find them.
4. Valley-fold all four petals down lightly.
5. Hold the stem firmly near the bottom and arrange the petals, curling them slightly by rolling them round a pencil. The diagram shows one petal down.
6. The Lily completed.

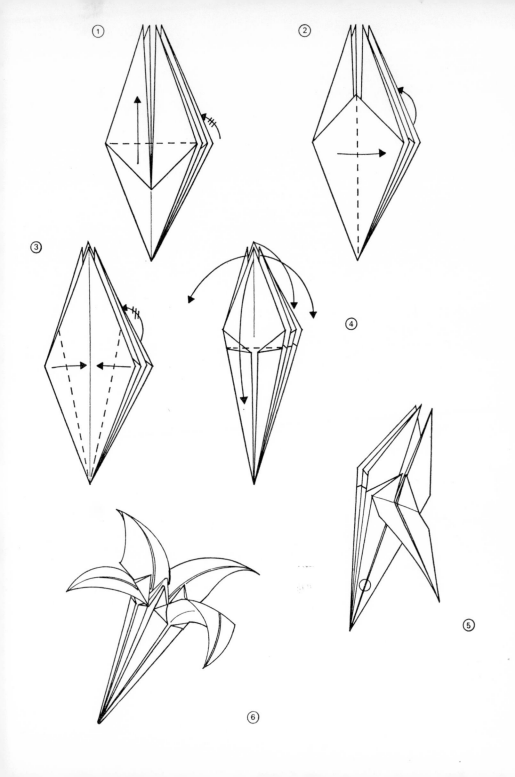

7

Models Made from the Handkerchief Base and the Water-bomb Base

---

Carp

1. Begin with the Handkerchief Base (Method 2, pages 22 and 23), using strong scarlet paper. Valley-fold flap A to the top.
2. Valley-fold both sides of the front leaf to the centre line.
3. Valley-fold the sides again to the centre line.
4. Fold down point A of top leaf. Turn over.
5. Petal-fold point B to the top (see pages 20 and 21).
6. Valley-fold both sides to the centre line.
7. Reverse-fold the two bottom points as you did with the frog's legs. Turn over.
8. Put your left index finger into the pocket behind flap A and hold the carp's mouth firmly between this finger and the left thumb. Put your right thumb between the loose edges of the Petal Fold at the back and the right index finger on the top. Pull the carp's head open gently as you did the body of the Crane (see pages 66 and 67).
9. The head is almost formed in this diagram. Continue to pull gently and work loose all the folds of the tail. Smooth out the body with finger and thumb. The head and the body should finally be in one long curve with the edges of the Petal Fold underneath meeting to make a tubular shape.
10. The Carp completed.

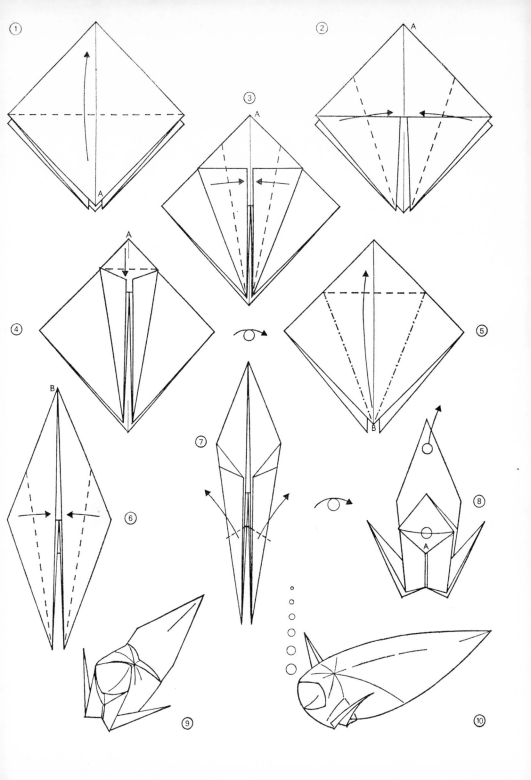

Water-bomb

1. Begin with the Water-bomb Base (see pages 18 and 19), open ends at the bottom. Valley-fold flaps A and B to the top. Repeat at the back with C and D.
2. Valley-fold E and F, front layers only, to the centre point X.
3. Valley-fold points A and B down. Repeat Step 2 at the back.
4. Valley-fold flaps A and B and tuck them into the two pockets shown by the arrows. Turn over and repeat with flaps C and D at the back.
5. Blow very hard where shown by the arrow.
6. The Water-bomb completed.

The Chinese call this a Paper Ball. It can be filled with water and hurled in furious fun at a wall or an enemy.

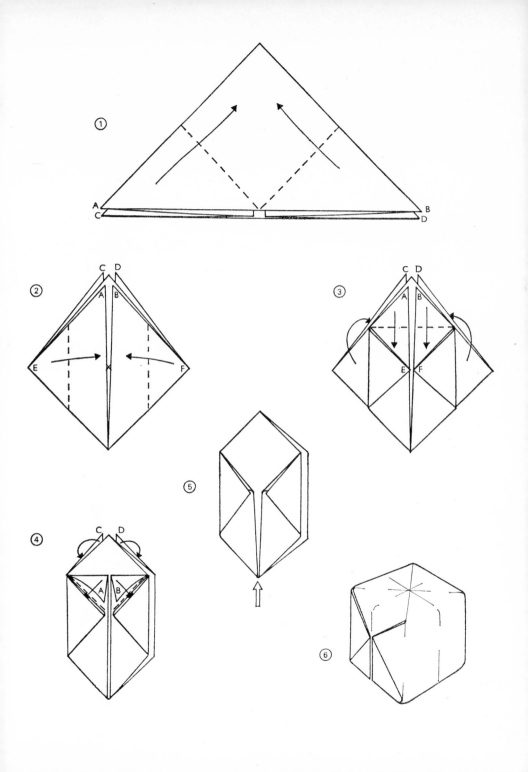

Chinese Pagoda

This is made with nine squares of paper of diminishing size. Each storey is made separately and then inserted into the one below. The squares must be cut and folded very accurately. To make a pagoda ten inches high, the squares should be 5, $4\frac{3}{4}$, $4\frac{1}{2}$, $4\frac{1}{4}$, 4, $3\frac{3}{4}$, $3\frac{1}{2}$, $3\frac{1}{4}$, 3 inches. You can make any size you like but the squares should diminish by about a quarter of an inch at a time. If you make a smaller one with the largest square having 3-inch sides, you can finally squash it flat and use it as a book-marker. The paper should then be very thin. Begin with the largest square and fold each square as follows.

1. Make a Water-bomb Base (see pages 18 and 19) with the open edges at the bottom. Valley-fold points A and B to the top. Repeat at the back.
2. Valley-fold A and B down to C along DE. Lift up point B, put your thumb between the edges of the triangle BEC and squash-fold into a square as in Diagram 3. Repeat on the left with triangle ADC. Turn over and repeat both folds at the back.
3. Valley-fold point A to D and point B to E. Repeat at the back.
4. Mountain-fold the top layer on both sides, taking the sides in between the two layers of the base. Repeat at the back.
5. Open out the top corners, while lifting the bottom flap, and squash flat. Repeat at the back.
6. One storey completed. Make all the other storeys in the same way.
7. Join the storeys in their right order of diminishing size by slipping the legs of the upper storey into the pockets of the lower one marked by the arrows. Push each storey well down so that the sloping edges meet.
8. The Pagoda completed.

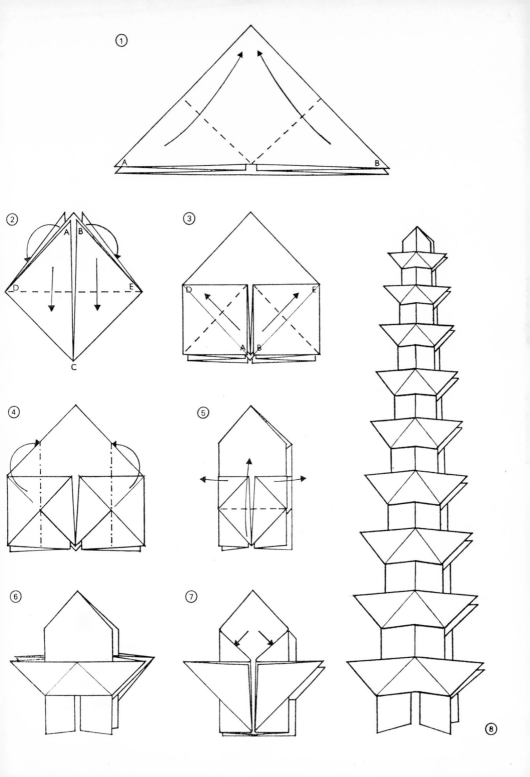